EARTHFORMS

LAKES

By Martha London

Consultant: Beth Gambro
Reading Specialist, Yorkville, Illinois

BEARPORT PUBLISHING

Minneapolis, Minnesota

Teaching Tips

Before Reading

- Look at the cover of the book. Discuss the picture and the title.
- Ask readers to brainstorm a list of what they already know about lakes. What can they expect to see in the book?
- Go on a picture walk, looking through the pictures to discuss vocabulary and make predictions about the text.

During Reading

- Read for purpose. Encourage readers to think about characteristics of lakes.
- Ask readers to look for the details of the book. Where does lake water come from?
- If readers encounter an unknown word, ask them to look at the sounds in the word. Then, ask them to look at the rest of the page. Are there any clues to help them understand?

After Reading

- Encourage readers to pick a buddy and reread the book together.
- Ask readers to name two ways people use lakes. Find the pages that tell about these uses.
- Ask readers to write or draw something they learned about lakes.

Credits
Cover and title page, © xphotoz/iStock; 3, © Willard/iStock; 5, © AscentXmedia/iStock; 7, © Adam Smigielski/iStock; 8–9, © DieterMeyrl/iStock; 11, © levers2007/iStock; 13, © Stanislav_Moroz/iStock; 15, © Sandra Burm/Shutterstock; 16–17, © BrianEKushner/iStock; 18, © andreswd/iStock; 19, © WHPics/iStock; 21, © jjshaw14/iStock; 22T, © pingebat/Shutterstock; 22M, © andreigilbert/iStock; 22B, © avdeev007/iStock; 23TL, © Srongkrod/iStock; 23TM, © GomezDavid/iStock; 23TR, © Shenki/iStock; 23BL, © Olena Lialina/iStock; 23BM, © Robert Ruidl/iStock; 23BR, © mammuth/iStock.

See BearportPublishing.com for our statement on Generative AI Usage.

Library of Congress Cataloging-in-Publication Data is available at www.loc.gov or upon request from the publisher.

ISBN: 979-8-89232-623-0 (hardcover)
ISBN: 979-8-89232-703-9 (paperback)
ISBN: 979-8-89232-663-6 (ebook)

Copyright © 2025 Bearport Publishing Company. All rights reserved. No part of this publication may be reproduced in whole or in part, stored in any retrieval system, or transmitted in any form or by any means, electronic, mechanical, photocopying, recording, or otherwise, without written permission from the publisher.

For more information, write to Bearport Publishing, 5357 Penn Avenue South, Minneapolis, MN 55419.

Contents

Watery World

Sunlight shines on the lake.

Small waves wash up on the sandy **shore**.

Let's jump into the water.

Splash!

What is a lake?

A lake is a big body of water.

It has land all around it.

There are lakes all over the world.

Most lakes formed many years ago.

Glaciers dug **valleys** into the ground.

They made big bowls in the land.

Lakes form when water fills the valleys.

Most lakes have fresh water.

Many plants and animals need this water to live.

A few lakes have **salt water**.

Where do lakes get water?

Rain falls and snow **melts**.

Rivers **flow** and carry water to some lakes.

Other lakes get water from under the ground.

Lakes are always changing.

Water hits the shore and dirt falls into the lake.

Then, dirt piles up on the lake bottom.

The lake gets smaller.

Many plants grow in and around lakes.

Fish swim through the plants.

Birds hunt for fish to eat.

People need lakes, too.

We drink the fresh water.

Farmers use the water to grow plants for food.

Lakes are fun.

People fish and go swimming in lakes.

Boats sail on the water.

Do you live near a lake?

Lake Baikal

Lake Baikal is the deepest lake in the world. Say it like bye-KAHL.

Lake Baikal is in Siberia, Russia.

This lake is home to the only freshwater seals on Earth.

Lake Baikal is deeper than most parts of the ocean.

Glossary

flow to move in a smooth, steady stream

glaciers large chunks of ice made of packed snow

melts changes from from solid to liquid with heat

salt water water with a lot of salt in it, such as ocean water

shore the land along the edge of a lake

valleys areas of lower land between hills or mountains

Index

Read More

Berne, Emma Carlson. *Underwater Animals (A Watery World).* Minneapolis: Bearport, 2025.

Regan, Lisa. *Lakes and Ponds (The Great Outdoors).* Buffalo, NY: Enslow, 2022.

Learn More Online

1. Go to **FactSurfer.com** or scan the QR code below.
2. Enter "**Earthforms Lakes**" into the search box.
3. Click on the cover of this book to see a list of websites.

About the Author

Martha London lives in Minnesota. She loves spending time outside.